A quick but useful perspective to effective leadership

Dr. Gregory Pace

ISBN 978-1-54398-395-1 eBook 978-1-54398-396-8

Contents

PROLOGUE

There I was, standing at "parade rest" (a position assumed by members of the military) in which the feet are 12 inches apart, the hands are clasped behind the back, and the head is held motionless and facing forward. Also, I did not forget to keep my legs straight without locking my knees, resting the weight of my body equally on the heels and balls of my feet. In this position, you must ask for permission to speak. This was the position I had assumed to listen to a senior leader tell me I "did not need a higher education past high school to follow orders in the military." The butt chewing continued with: "If the military had wanted me to have a degree, then they would have recruited me straight after college, or I would have joined as a commissioned officer." This experience just motivated me to prove this individual wrong.

Fast forward three years later, I am now placed in a leadership role at the young age of 21. The question some might ask: did I adopt the leadership philosophy of that senior leader? In short, no: I not only encouraged civilian education amongst my soldiers, but I also led the charge by setting the example for the individuals whom I was fortunate enough to mentor and lead. I also learned that the senior enlisted promotion board frowned when they reviewed the records of enlisted members with college degrees.

It would appear that I was spending too much time focused on professional development instead of taking care of the soldiers. However, I will let my successful military career prove this falsehood. I not only focused on civilian education, but I also maxed out on military education, physical fitness, military awards, and weapons qualification. As previously stated, the negativity just motivated me to prove these individuals wrong.

Now it is eight years later. I am in Grafenwoehr, Germany, and I have achieved the rank of Sergeant First Class (the first rank where you have entered the rank of senior noncommissioned officer). I was fortunate enough to serve in the role of platoon sergeant. From this experience, I could share with you numerous leadership challenges (ineffective leadership), but I will focus instead on the positive leadership since this is a leadership book. But, as previously, I was able to turn negativity into positivity.

Now let's fast forward to 23 years later, as I retired from the active military. For my first job after retiring from the military, I decided to become a Junior Reserve Officer Training Corps Instructor. This was the opportunity to take all my leadership experience and training and attempt to mold and guide future leaders. The catch was that most of my students, still in high school, did not know about leadership or want to lead, and they certainly didn't want to listen to who they called an "old army guy."

My intent after retirement was to spend time with my daughters, to give back to my family after the sacrifices they had made while I was serving in the military. Unfortunately, my wife was not able to transfer her job to the location where I was teaching, so I had to break the news to my students that I was leaving. That was one of the most difficult leadership decisions that I had to make, but the students (some of whom I now call friends) truly understood.

My next role was to get a job with the federal government. What a mistake. I will not mention the name of the organization, but I could not believe this was the federal government, one of the only agencies that is supposed to support veterans. This was a place that was infested with bad leadership, literally a walking nightmare. The leadership or I would say lack of leadership made me question my leadership abilities every day of my three years there. But we are often placed in situations for a reason. I guess the reason for this challenge was to let me appreciate the power of positive leadership.

I want to tell you that the environment was so toxic that I started getting headaches when I walked through the door. That poor leadership contributed directly to high turnover, absenteeism, and who knows what other ills. I am not just complaining; this toxic environment can be fact-checked in the newspaper and online.

If it wasn't for my military background, true friends, and previous dealings with ineffective leadership, this would have been the first job I ever quit. I remember one day I got so frustrated that I got very sick and foolishly drove home (60 miles). Fortunately, one friend called me and talked to me all the way to the house. That friend used the power of positive leadership.

I am finally in a job with the federal government where I am valued as an individual and as an employee. The work environment is 180 degrees different from the previous job. This job values the opinion of each and every employee.

Now that I have gone down memory lane and shared with you my plight for leadership development, let me get to the main reason I wrote this book. The remaining chapters or inspirational quotes should help you in your leadership journey. However, I want you to challenge yourself to see if you know when to Lead, Follow, or just Get Out of the Way.

1

Introduction

This book was written to give you a real-world perspective and application of when to lead, follow, or just get out of the way. I have witnessed both effective and ineffective leadership throughout my journey of trying to understand why some leaders excel and why others fail. My understanding of this topic is supported through 23 years of military service, over six years federal government service, and two years of public service (teaching high school Junior Reserve Officer Training Corps (JROTC). I am also an Adjunct Professor, where I have contributed directly to educating future leaders from junior college to graduate school. This has provided me with over 30 years of leading and following in numerous organizations. However, for you to get a better understand of my thought process, I would like to share my meaning of leading and following. Throughout this book leadership is defined as the art of guiding an individual or group to achieve the stated objective of the organization. The "art" in this context is mentoring, coaching, training, developing, listening, counseling, and communicating. Followership, which I truly believe carries equal weight as leadership, is defined as the art of being led. The "art" consists of listening, learning, understanding, and communicating. Communication is the critical component that connects both leadership and followership. I cannot express strongly enough the importance of having effective communication throughout an organization.

I have often heard that "leaders are born." I believe people are born with the characteristic traits to learn to be a leader, but some individuals develop that skill set a lot faster than others. That said, although some individuals seem to be genetically designed to follow, I don't want those individuals to follow blindly. This is where I introduce my leadership philosophy of "trust but verify." A key and very effective role of a good follower is to verify that the actions of the leader are consistent with that of an effective leader. The structure of this book is divided into three primary components that are essential to your passage of becoming an effective leader. The title of the book should give you a hint about that structure.

You may be asking yourself now: how do I get there from here? As we navigate through this book, I want you to keep these three topics in the forefront of your minds:

1. Do not let your past determine your future; however,
2. Remember your past to prevent you from repeating similar mistakes; and
3. Never forget from whence you came.

Some may be a little confused, but by the end of this book, it should be clear. Now let's take a dive into the first one.

Do Not Let Your Past Determine Your Future

The primary intent of this statement is to focus you on moving forward to achieve success, keeping in mind that success is how you define it. Now ask yourself: If I allowed my past to determine my future, where would I be? Neither of my parents finished high school, yet they instilled in me the motivation and drive to continue moving forward, regardless of the obstacles that were placed in front of me. Honestly, I would not be sharing my thoughts and tip(s) with you, let alone having achieved my doctorate. Growing up, I had several paths that were laid before me: a paved road, a paved road with potholes, and a dirt road (which turned to mud in the Mississippi rain of my childhood). I can clearly remember the travels I took on that paved road with potholes, yet I still made it to where I am today. Let me break this down so you can understand the context. Your "past" are the travels that you took to get to where you are today.

I reference the "past" because we cannot turn back time to repeat those steps. The roads are the choice(s) we make or are forced to travel. I will explain. The "paved road" is what we see as the ideal choice, which includes no obstacles, a great support team, and continuous positive encouragement. The "paved road with potholes" is similar to the paved road, but has some obstacles that make for a less smooth but not an impossible journey. Next is the "dirt road," as I referred to—thick as "Mississippi Mud." This last path is tough to navigate; your support group (if you even have one) is not encouraging, and if you continue to travel this path, it often leads to a dead end (no pun intended). Your "future" is the travel yet to come. With that said, think about where you are now, how you got here, and where you are planning to go.

Remembering your past to avoid repeating similar mistakes is one of the hallmarks of learning and developing as a leader. One of my leadership philosophies is that it is okay to make a mistake as long as you don't keep repeating the same mistake. I would be lying to you if I said that all of my leadership decisions were effective the first time. Lastly, I mentioned never forget from whence you came. Some leaders tend to forget that they were once a follower and get caught up in the trap that "I am the leader; therefore, I demand loyalty."

Effective leadership is one of the essential characteristics that people look for when choosing to stay or join an organization. This occurs when individuals choose for themselves that they are going to follow the direction and guidance of someone else. Bottom line: it is an intentional act to follow leaders that effectively communicate the vision of the organization.

2

Leadership Theories

Researchers both current and past have established theoretical frameworks of leadership through the use of various definitions. However, the majority of leadership theories tend to focus on Bass's theory of transformational approach (1990), House's theory of charismatic approach, and most recently the adaptive leadership styles of Hackman and Wageman. Keep in mind that an effective leadership combination consists of a blend of several leadership styles that are adaptable to various situations, although I have read numerous articles that argue against using multiple leadership approaches or components of different styles in similar situations to avoid inconsistency. The potential problem with that viewpoint is a leader dedicated to one leadership style remains inflexible and unable to function in situations where their style is not producing positive results. Northouse's (2004) work attempts to direct leaders to apply various leadership theories to current global organizations' situations. Northouse's research introduces the components of leadership with an examination of several theories and concludes with a dialogue focusing on the transformation process theory.

This research furthers differentiates role and responsibility of leaders by virtue of their formal and informal positions as viewed by the employees within the organization. Individual attributes, competencies, and leadership outcomes are some of the contributing environmental impacts that enhances a leader's capabilities to lead effectively and influence employees' performance (Mumford et al., 2000). This model's emphasis is directed toward improving abilities and knowledge to mold effective leaders.

I limited the majority of my research to the previous decade except for the current research conducted on adaptive leadership. This book will enhance the leadership theories by focusing on several skills that affect individuals throughout organizations. When I served in the military, it was in a transition to adopt a new leadership style known as adaptive leadership following the recent conflicts to combat terrorism. These recent conflicts have made it possible to study post wartime results of implementing leadership theories in relationship to their impact on followers and organizational retention.

An effective leader is required to solve simple and complex problems that occur within the organization. This shift in thinking includes not only implementing existing leadership theories but also innovatively developing practical solutions throughout (Mumford et al., 2000). Achieving these tasks requires an understanding of the available leadership theories in practice and application. There were several leadership theories used by the United States Army including those of other civilian leaders during my time of service. During my doctoral studies, I conducted research that looked at the correlational relationship amongst transformational, transactional, charismatic, cognitive resource, and adaptive leadership styles as a component that affected a soldier's decision to remain on active duty.

Transformational Leadership Theory

Transformational leadership style allows leaders the ability to capitalize on the talent and experience their subordinates already have within themselves to accomplish a given task. This style in certain scenarios can be effective when the leader communicates a task to the subordinates and then steps back and allows the followers to execute. Transformational leadership, on the other hand, will most likely achieve positive outcomes in organizations that embrace change, meaning that success will most likely be achieved when there is a demand that requires a change, or the organization is in a period where new opportunities are frequently prevalent.

Transformational leadership style is designed to work appropriately in unstable organizations that require immediate intervention. However, this leadership style may be ineffective when the organization lacks the experience needed in the workers, or the situation allows no flexibility to transition from established procedures or processes. Transformational style leadership challenges subordinates to think outside their normal paradigm. Nevertheless, research has shown that transformational leadership contributes to the development of both leaders and followers. This development is mostly geared toward the follower in terms of self-esteem and commitment. Within this process, the leader may identify other means of accomplishing a given task. Leadership styles typically encompass limitation(s); a constant use of this style can minimize the ability to continue to influence followers.

Transactional Leadership Theory

The transactional style of leadership is based on rewarding followers for an acceptable performance. Some leaders opt not to use this style because of the negative stigma associated with it. A leader could use this style to enforce the role of safety. For example, the leadership provides a reward for employee safety during the accomplishment of a specific task. If the acceptable performance continues, success is achieved. However, if the employee fails to maintain, it is possible he or she will see the leadership as self –centered. Reliance on a transactional style alone has the propensity to limit opportunities for self-growth as a follower because of limited room for errors.

An experienced leader empowers subordinates through the process of building a strong functional organization. Using this perspective, subordinates learn best by doing, as a leader often accepts structured risks and takes responsibility for the potential mistakes of the inexperienced subordinates. Organizations tend to be productive when leaders establish trust and build confidence in subordinates, allowing them to learn through experience.

Charismatic Leadership Theory

Choi (2006) states, "charismatic leadership is assumed to have three core components: envisioning, empathy, and empowerment. A charismatic leader's envisioning behavior influences followers' need for achievement and the leader's empathic behavior stimulates followers' need for affiliation." Charismatic leadership, like transformational leadership, empowers followers to make decisions with direct guidance. Both theories require experienced subordinates, effective communications, and consideration on behalf of the leader.

Choi (2006) also expresses, "one of the most important determinates of your effectiveness as a leader, coach, and mentor is success in positively influencing others. We all have influencing skills; the crucial question is whether those skills results in a high level of commitment and are helpful and strengthen the other person." You will always hear me say that leading is about influencing others. Leaders establish objectives and motivate followers to successfully accomplish them by providing motivation and purpose. Leaders must be effective communicators. Effective communication is measured through the establishment of a common or shared agreement between the leader and follower.

Cognitive Resource Theory

The cognitive resource theory, according to Fiedler (1986): "the leader has a directive style and subordinates require guidance in order to perform" (p. 540). In this leadership style, leaders direct what objectives will be completed and how they will be performed. This style is preferred in a new work environment, where subordinates lack the experience to perform without immediate guidance. According to Fiedler, an intelligent leader devises strategies to improve performance when faced with a complex task that leads to increased.

In "What Leaders Really Do," Kotter states people in battle must be led and that no one has developed a successful formula of management" (p. 86). People, regardless of the situation, need the motivation and inspiration that comes from a leader who can clearly and eloquently articulate the vision and direction of the organization along with the purpose and mission that drives them. Nevertheless, the leader must also possess the skills of a manager who has a well-developed plan of attack. Kotter's research also highlighted that some organizations are often "over-managed" and "under-led"; however; he also states the key is developing a combination of tough leadership and management to create a balance to the organization and that "smart companies" value both kinds of people" (p. 86). In its simplest definition, effective leadership in an organization requires procedures in place to cope with complexity and change.

Gilley, Gilley, and McMillan (2009), present several other variables that impact leaders' effectiveness in leading. The study examined the efficiency of leadership in adapting to organizational transformation. These findings established a link in confirming previous studies that associated effective change skills with specific leadership behavior when implementing change in an organization. According to this study, two associated factors are motivation and communication. The previous mentioned factors possibly can be a contributing factor in retention within an organization.

Acknowledgement from leaders that change is not avoidable increases an organization's chances of success tremendously. When an organization is willing to embrace change, it often emerges better than when it started. Leadership tends to encompass the management of change, making it work for the organization. Finally, research has shown that despite the variety of views on leadership types, all leadership ultimately reduce to a dyadic relation between leaders and followers.

Character and Morale of Leaders

Variances exist concerning the traditional leadership characteristics and morale building between leaders of various organizations. Military leaders are trained to apply leadership principles to various situations until the art of leading is embedded; this is a method of training not education (Kezar, Carducci, & Contreras-McGavin, 2006). Decision-making in the military sometimes leads to critical consequences compared to outcomes in civilian life. However, both civilian and military leadership share characteristics that encompass the principle of decision-making and effective communication strategies. Again, the term "effective communications" is prevalent in almost every discussion. This discussion could be introducing leadership or just following a person in the position of leadership.

Morale is a principal component to the success or failure of both military and civilian organizations. Britt (2003) implies that subordinates will become apathetic toward the organization if they discover that their employment lacks significance. Hence, maintaining high morale within an organization is critical.

There are numerous philosophies for refining morale within organizations. The significance of my research focused on leaders understanding the importance of establishing and maintaining high morale in their organizations. However, regardless of the type of organization, leaders must develop this skill to be truly successful.

According to Hersey, Blanchard, and Johnson (2008), "managers need to devote time to nurture the leadership potential, motivation, morale, climate, commitment to objectives, decision-making skills, communication skills, and problem-solving skills to their people. Thus, an important role of managers is the development of the task-relevant performance readiness of their followers" (p. 236). This style of leadership has been proven to be equally effective in the United States, Europe, and Asia. The use of this leadership style when put into application can be effective leading (military and civilian) alike. Now that you have been armed with my background and leadership perspective, let's dive into the identification and application of leading, following, and knowing when it is time to step aside.

3

Lead

Leadership development is the preparation of leaders through training, education, experience, assessment, counseling, and (do not forget) feedback. Effective leaders grow potential leaders at all levels or ranks within their organizations. I have learned leadership development is purposeful, not accidental. Some leaders go out of their way to mentor, guide, and shape future leaders. Effective leaders can influence others to accomplish a desired outcome. Motivating others to follow you is not always an easy task to accomplish, but effective leadership abilities make this task achievable.

Leaders come in different forms and have different traits, styles, goals, and philosophies. Becoming an influential leader requires an understanding and demonstration in the areas of critical thinking, forecasting, leading change, interpersonal relationships, ethics, communication, negotiation, and leadership principles. My studies have given me a better understanding in each of these areas and have taught me that there is no one right answer when it comes to developing leadership skills.

As a former Sergeant Major (highest senior enlisted rank achievable in the United States Army), I spent a great deal of time counseling and guiding soldiers due to bad behavior and to foster improvement. The success of these encounters relied heavily on effective communication (I don't want to leave out listening) and trust building. In many cases, it served me better to effectively listen instead of just counseling them. Paying attention to non-verbal cues also improved my effectiveness, as there are times people tell you one thing, but their expressions are saying something else. While seeking to become an effective leader, one skill everyone can improve on is effective listening. For me, I take a bit more time listening or re-reading an item to try and get a deeper comprehension of what was written instead of pressing forward with my first impression of the message. I find this is ironic, as we are often taught to speed-read and listen only for key points, which I think can limit our ability to absorb the entirety of a message.

Merging a group of people to achieve a united objective can be difficult, but when you add in bad leadership, it is almost impossible. When you are combining a group of people toward one goal, those goals need to be understood from the top down. Communication is key on all fronts, and when there is a lack of communication, there will be issues. A skilled leader is needed in these types of situations. Once you have a good leader in place, it is just a matter of supporting them and watching over their progress. When you have the right combination of leadership and follower-ship, great things can happen.

Research has been conducted to identify specific characteristics that predict the likelihood of success in a leadership role. However, I would like to state that this alone doesn't adequately assure effective leadership. Again, I want to reinforce that the use of a combination of leadership styles is needed to be effective.

In the end, it is not enough for me to be a good leader. Leaders should always be on the lookout for other up-and-coming leaders to develop and mentor. One of the best ways I have learned to accomplish this is to have a vision, be credible by leading by example, and communicate your message effectively. This approach lays the groundwork to be a great mentor and leader. I have often thought, what good is intelligence quotient (IQ) without common sense (CS)? This is extremely relevant to your development as a leader and follower. In other words, you can be smart (book smart), but if you do not know how to effectively apply what you have learned, you are not meeting your true potential.

Affiliative leadership: This leadership style encourages harmony within the organization. The leader is better equipped to help solve conflict through team-building. This leader is everyone's friend, focuses on developing relationships, building a nurturing atmosphere, and brings harmony to an organization. This leader is so well liked, people feel compelled to perform and deliver. The flip side to this style of leadership is the challenge of those who are not willing to participate; non-performers often remain within the organization for an extended period before being coached or terminated.

Authoritative leadership: An authoritative leader provides guidance and directions but allows subordinates the flexibility to accomplish the task(s) using their own approach. A leader that displays this leadership style is also known as a Command and Control Leader. This individual is needed in an organization that lacks direction and focus. In retrospect, this is the leader that is required to develop, motivate the people, and execute plans to accomplish the vision. This leadership style is very helpful in organizations that are autonomous (single-focused organizations), but not so much in organizations that have dependencies outside of their own organization) and don't require cross-team collaboration.

Charismatic leadership: This leader leads through the power of charisma. They inspire with their presence and can elevate the morale of their team. The charismatic leader energizes success by creating the sense of commitment to the organization from their trust. The risk, however, is once this leader leaves, individuals and teams lose the rallying point around which they assembled. This could cause the team to underdeliver or not deliver at all.

Coercive leadership: Coercive leadership focuses employees on immediate problems, with little or no input; it is a key leadership style when dealing with a problem employee or a critical situation. Characteristics displayed can consist of leading with an iron fist; having all the answers to the plan for executing a winning strategy; no room for alternative solutions; and solicitation of feedback is at a minimum or nonexistent. This type of leadership is found in a toxic environment. Nevertheless, a leader of this nature when introduced to a team in crisis could be just the leader that is needed to save a sinking ship. Yet, once the ship is back on course and tracking, this type of leader should be replaced, as those on the ship might stage a mutiny.

Coaching leadership: Coaching leadership style concentrates on the professional and personal development of the followers. This style of leadership requires self-aware followers. This leader invests in their people. This style is effective when leading younger, ambitious charges that are invested in developing personal and professional skills needed to be successful in future endeavors. The Coach Leader, however, would not be as successful with a group of tenured charges that are riding out the last of their working days until retirement.

Democratic leadership: This type of leader lead by consensus. This is possible when the leader does not have the expertise to make decisions on their own but relies on the expertise of their staff to assist in the decision-making process. Organizations that are resistant to change and which in turns require a large majority of buy-in and commitment could benefit from this style of leadership. This style is not effective in times of crisis when immediate decisions are required.

Innovative leadership: The Innovative Leader is a champion of embracing new ideas and leading change. The Innovative Leader faces failure head-on and is seen as an individual that encourages failure to discover success. The team flourishes because they feel valued by the organization and can "think outside the box." As with any leadership style, this style carries a higher degree of risk. However, a vast reward could be had if the ideas are solid.

Laissez-faire leadership: This leader experiences success because of the people that they allow within their circle and/or surround themselves with. This leader is an effective communicator and receptive to giving and receiving feedback as often as possible. The risk of the Laissez-faire Leader comes from the trusting nature of the style. If the leader's trust is betrayed, it may take some time for the leader to realize it, by which time, the organization could be in trouble.

Pacesetting leadership: The Pacesetting Leader establishes high performance standards within the organization. The leader sets the ideal behavior for other members to follow; however, the leader provides limited to no feedback to assist the team. This leadership style works when the leader has highly talented and motivated individuals from within the organization working for a common goal. Consequently, this type of leader poses a negative effect on organizations where individuals don't measure up to their expectations or true potential. This approach can generate anger, subversion, and trust issues amongst the workers being held to unreasonable expectations.

Passive-avoidant leadership: The passive-avoidant style of leader intervenes when the situation focus is on noncompliance of an established standard or when the situation requires a leadership action that has previously occurred within the organization (Yukl, 2004).

Servant leadership: This leader puts the needs of the team or organization before the needs of self. Servant Leaders include each member of the team in the decision-making process, provide the tools necessary to getting the job done, take responsibility when things do not go well, and share the credit when things go right. The downside to Servant Leadership is that in pressured situations when decisions need to be made quickly, this leader can often struggle.

Transactional leadership: Transactional leadership is an incentive-based leadership style. Employees' performance and commitment to the organization's goals are based on the notion that the leader who leads, manages, and directs his or her employees or followers provides incentives for the subordinates' accomplishment of the task(s) (Yukl, 2004).

Transformational leadership: Transformational style leadership predicts situational awareness, and this effect seems to rest on the facet of intellectual stimulation. Leaders who master this form of leadership connect with their followers through effective communication of the leader's intent (Yukl, 2004).

As I stated earlier, there are a lot of different styles. This list has been a sample of a much larger set of styles that are available, not to mention the hybrids where aspects from two or more are combined to navigate scenarios where a single style does not fit.

Leadership Tips

Learning to lead is not an easy road to travel. However, the rewards of becoming an effective leader, listener, mentor, follower, and communicator outweigh its trials and tribulations. One should not expect to become a leader overnight, but should prepare to lead daily. I encourage you to find a mentor to help you develop your leadership skills. Keep in mind that mentorship is reciprocal, so be careful who you choose as a mentor. I believe that inspire is to encourage not discourage. However, both words end with courage. So even if I discourage you from doing the wrong thing, I still have inspired you through my courage.

The three characteristics of leadership are vision, credibility, and communication competence. A leader develops a vision then enables the energy from their group/followers to carry out and accomplish that vision. When a follower respects their leader, the leader receives five bases of power: competence, character, composure, sociability, and extroversion.

The leader must also articulate their vision in a way that their team understands and buys into.

Furthermore, the leader must recognize where the group struggles and succeeds to establish guidelines and rules and to develop a new path for those they lead. Since leadership is a function of a system, I learned that leadership could be adapted and customized based on the goal, the team, and the mission. People are a leader's greatest assets. A successful leader learns how to manage the group dynamics so that the execution of the mission is smooth, and the followers are happy. That is when you win as a leader.

I once learned that leadership is not about titles or positions. It is about one life influencing another. After over 20 years of serving in various leadership roles in the military and being elected head of several organizations, I don't worry about what title I have or what position I am categorized in, or any job for that matter. All I want to do is influence change in people while working on a common goal for any organization. Keeping that in mind as a leader you must communicate, listen, act, and serve in the capacity that will create positive direction for your organization. The people that you lead deserve your best as a leader.

Leadership is paramount in establishing a critical path toward success for any organization. The leader's role is establishing and setting forth the vision and communicating that vision to the organization. The leader also plays an integral part in executing the vision by promoting standards and values by which the organizational operates. Leadership, in my opinion, is a group of characteristics or traits that anyone in the organization may display.

You don't have to be in a position of power to be a leader. One simply must choose to lead, as they see fit. A good leader, at any level of the organization, will have a clear understanding of the vision and mission. They will have a full understanding of the cultural and education background of the individuals they lead to enable them to better communicate the vision to everyone in a way they may best understand it. Good leaders create an environment where employees feel protected, which ultimately encourages them to fully invest themselves in the vision.

Leaders have the great opportunity to influence others in so many ways. As a leader, I know personally that I can influence others by leading from the front, not asking to do something I would not do myself. Nevertheless, don't show favoritism and remember what you do for one, you must do for everyone else. As a leader, you can influence others by taking the lead and leading by example. Stay the course and don't let your position of authority get the best of you. Leaders often forget that part of their role is to influence instead of demand. Influence requires interaction with others, which contributes directly to effective leadership.

Trust but Verify

People tend to follow individuals that they trust. The verification is completed by the actions demonstrated by the leader. The takeaway from my leadership philosophy is that "leadership requires a relationship" between the leader and follower. The leader's role is to establish trust, and the follower's role is to verify that the actions of the leader are genuine. This is a universal tip for both leadership and follower-ship.

Leaders undoubtedly must be effective communicators with their organization on various levels. However, communicating across the human spectrum is a challenge within itself. All organizations must recognize this obstacle and implement methods to reduce the friction. It is helpful to establish a personal and professional presence in communicating between leaders and their followers. Today's millennials are technologically knowledgeable; therefore, technology is an important aspect of leading them into the future. With the increased use of technology, leaders must be aware and supportive of the different methods of communication. Modern technology can help people communicate more effectively and prevent communication conflict.

4

Follow

Here is a question that has puzzled some for years, "What makes a Leader?" This can also be phrased as, "What makes a person want to follow?" I would venture to answer these as: motivation, empathy, and social skills. These qualities in some eyes are considered "soft" characteristics. There is much more involved than these characteristics in becoming either a successful leader or an effective follower. Both must have a genuine, emotional connection with people to be successful. Now to take it a step further, the follow-up question is, "What makes an effective leader or follower?" Again, numerous things come to mind. Fill in the blank______, ______.

Relationship Between Followership and Leadership Styles and their Traits

Followership and leadership: Which comes first? Can you really have one without the other? Not likely. If you have followers, does that mean you're a leader? It is possible. It certainly is true that an effective leader has followers. For years I have studied the question, do we find the same correlation between leadership and followership? Do different types of followers require different types of leaders? Experts and my experience say "yes." The leadership style that one might adopt is dependent upon the type of followers one has. The Situational Leadership Model (Hersey, Blanchard & Johnson) is a well-known model that is used to determine which leadership approach one should employ based on the type of followers one has. The ultimate belief of the situational leadership model is that there is no single "best" style of leadership.

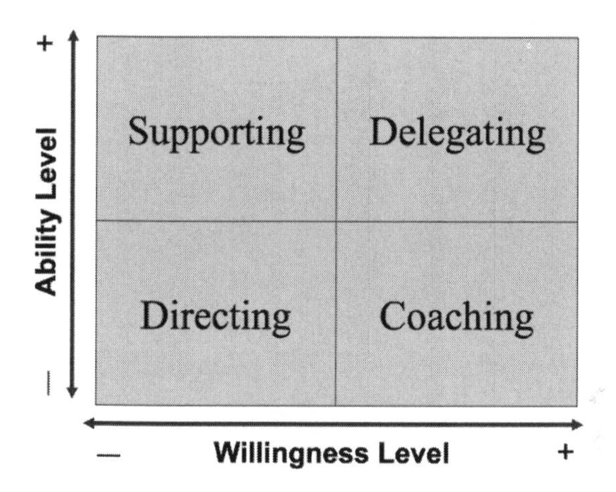

As ability and willingness level increase, the more autonomy a follower will have and the less involvement will be necessary on the part of the leader. The opposite is also true, as ability and willingness decrease, the less autonomy the follower will have, and the more involvement will be required on the part of the leader. I will attempt to explain this further as we look at these methods more meticulously.

Directing

A directing style of leadership is needed when the follower is unskilled or lacks the confidence or motivation to achieve the task(s). There may also be a level of risk involved with the task(s) that requires direct monitoring during execution. If a leader does not assume this method of leadership with an unskilled and unmotivated follower, the likelihood for success is borderline, at best. Followers that require this type of leadership might be categorized as troubled or challenged and are commonly on a performance improvement plan.

Coaching

A coaching style of leadership is needed when the follower lacks the skill needed to perform the task(s) but has a high confidence or motivation to complete them. This allows the follower the opportunity to learn and improve their ability to complete the given task(s). Followers that require this type of leadership could be categorized as young and ambitious; however, it is not age dependent.

Supporting

A leader having to assume a supporting role would do so when the follower can do the job but lacks the motivation. I have found this approach has been required when a follower has had a life event that creates distractors. Your understanding of what is causing the lack of motivation is crucial in resolving the issue. A leader practicing the supporting role understands that skills and processes are not the issue and works to reveal the motivational issues. This will also occur if the follower has experienced failure and simply needs some positive encouragement to improve their confidence. Typically, the leader assumes the role of a counselor by listening to the follower, offering supportive praise, and building confidence.

Delegating

This is the optimal leadership role to take. A leader assumes the delegating role when the follower has high skill and high motivation. These types of followers are typically the leaders' star employees. Leaders operating within the delegation role allow a great use of independence for this follower to execute the task(s). In this scenario, the followers exercise sound judgment, exceptional critical thinking, and high levels of effective communication.

Each interaction between a leader and their followers subjects the leader to the possibility of employing a different leadership style. As you will learn, there is no one solution (approach) that will satisfy all encounters. A leader must be flexible and knowledgeable to truly understand the circumstances that contribute to the interaction (leader follower relationship). The leader must then adjust their leadership style to match the needs of the follower and the situation, in general. To this end, there are numerous leadership styles identified.

This raises the question, if there are numerous leadership styles, are there numerous followership styles, as well? Yes, there are. In addition to the four follower styles noted in the Situational Leadership Model, there are numerous followership styles that exist.

Alienated followership: These followers believe their way is always better than that of their leader. These followers often question the leader in a passive-aggressive manner. These individuals are highly independent thinkers, but do not engage in discussions while they are taking place, choosing to be critical after the fact to their friends. This type of follower can undermine the efforts of a leader and should be addressed immediately, once discovered.

Exemplary or effective followership: These followers are free-thinking, good decision-making, and highly effective workers. They have a high level of initiative and participate in the processes that formulate action. These followers are often identified in succession plans for future promotion opportunities.

Passive followership: These followers would fall in the lower-left half of the Situational Leadership model. These followers lack the motivation, drive, and engagement to be high-performing employees. These followers require a very high level of engagement on the part of the leader and, ultimately, detract from the mission.

Pragmatic followership: These followers follow the leader with little resistance. Occasionally, they will question their leader, but only cursorily. They are moderately engaging and abstemiously independent. They will have occasional flashes of high performance, but even those are tempered by mediocrity. Overall, these workers are steady and reliable, but are not going to blow your socks off.

In this chapter, I have identified the relationship that exists between follower and leader. This was to demonstrate how different types of followers can influence their leaders' leadership style and vice versa. Additionally, I have identified a myriad of varying leadership and followership styles, with brief descriptions of each. What type of follower are you? Have you contributed to the organization or are you part of the problem that prevents progress within your organization?

Followership Tips

Individuals, regardless of what kind of leader or follower they are still need motivation, inspiration, and constructive feedback that comes from a leader who follows and establishes clear guidelines. Leaders should be able to clearly and articulately communicate a clear vision and desired direction of the organization. A leader must also possess the skills of a manager who has a well-developed plan to handle multiple situations as they occur.

One should first learn to be a follower before assuming a role of leadership. The skills, patience, and traits gained while following an effective leader can be very beneficial to you once you have assumed the role of leading. I am a true believer that we learn from our mistakes; however, success is achieved quickly if you can learn from the mistakes of others through mentorship. I can honestly share with you that I have learned from both good and bad leaders throughout my journey as a student (follower) of leadership. With the bad leader, I learned what not to do once I was placed in the leadership role. On the other hand, I adopted and utilized similar characteristics from the good leaders to become the individual I am today.

What Obstacles in Your Life Are Holding You Back from Triumph?

The "leader leads" and is responsible for the followers. The follower will follow their leader if their leader is honest, trustworthy, selfless, rewarding, empowering, and anything else the leader can be to show and draw loyalty to and from their followers. The leader and follower need one another to have success in an organization, mission, etc. Followers must be team players and want to part of the solution and not part of the problem. When a follower understands and is committed toward the direction that the leader wants to move, then and only then will they be part of the decision-making process. A follower and leader must be one and cannot be independent; they must rely on each other 100 per cent of the time, with the understanding that they still must be different or unique in their own way. If we were all the same, there would not be a need for someone else, because they would have the same idea and thought process. The great thing about a unit, everyone has a different idea of how they want to do things and can express their ideas and have a better product, but we must remember that the leader leads.

To have an effective organization and be an effective leader, leaders must have a great relationship with our followers (employees). Both leaders and followers must have trust in one another. Without faith, trust, and teamwork any of these, along with other values that have been established within the organization, your organization can be broken, weakened, or even just be the norm like many other organizations that are the status quo. We all must be a follower first; this is the preparatory step to becoming a leader.

How we think we are as a leader and how others see us as a leader are just some of the traits of leadership. There are numerous books and studies that give us ideas (traits) of how we are supposed to act as a leader. As we mature and experience life, we are put into situations where we must lead or follow. Those of us that choose to lead must use the traits of those that have led before us. As we progress through our leadership journey and start to mentor those that will soon follow, we must make sure to teach and use the right traits. One thing to remember is that the traits for one leader may not work for another (us). Next, I would like you to think about the following. What defines moral leadership from immoral leadership? Hint: A moral leader focuses more on the outcome(s) of achieving success for the entire organization, hence less focus on oneself.

5

Get Out of The Way

The true testament of an effective leader is knowing when to get out of the way of others that are trying to lead. Acknowledgment that you are becoming ineffective is not a sign of weakness but characteristic of a true leader.

When I was served in the United States Army, I led by example and challenged everyone who was under my direct leadership to excel and often mentored others that sought out my guidance and friendship. Let me take the time to share with you some of the accomplishments that were achieved, then I will let you be the judge of the leadership characteristics displayed.

My section was awarded the **V Corps Small Distinguished Unit Award** under my leadership by excelling in the following tasks.

Army Physical Fitness Badge: Soldiers who obtain a minimum score of 270 or above, with a minimum of 90 points per event on the Army Physical Fitness Test (APFT) and meet the body fat standards will be awarded the Physical Fitness Badge for Physical Fitness Excellence.

Expert Weapon Qualification: Soldiers must hit 23 to 29 out of the 40 targets to earn the marksmanship qualification. If you do a little better (30 to 35), you qualify for the sharpshooter badge. To get an expert badge, you must hit 36 to 40 of the targets.

No disciplinary Actions: the title itself requires no definition.

Dual Fixed Base (Air Traffic Control) and Tactical (Air Traffic Control) Certification: Each member is certified to control air traffic in peace time and combat.

Sergeant Morales Club (SMC): Members exemplify a special kind of leadership characterized by a personal concern for the needs, training, development, and welfare of soldiers. SMC membership recognizes and rewards distinguished NCOs whose leadership achievements merit special recognition and who have contributed significantly to developing a professional NCO Corps and a combat-effective army. This platoon had two members of the club.

Civilian education (working toward college education): All of the soldiers were enrolled and taking college courses in their spare time while serving in the armed forces.

Military education: All of the soldiers enrolled in training is a process which intends to establish and improve the capabilities of military personnel in their respective roles.

Master Fitness Trainer: The Master Fitness Trainer Course trains selected Noncommissioned Officers (NCOs) and Commissioned Officers in all aspects of the army's Physical Readiness Training (PRT) System, so they can be unit advisors on physical readiness issues and monitor the unit and individual physical readiness program. This platoon had two certified Master Fitness Trainers.

Bottom line: this platoon and the leadership within was so great that often I would drive into work thinking about what I wanted them to do. By the time I got to work, they were already doing "what I was thinking." So as a responsible leader I went to the First Sergeant and told him I needed to move. The question to some was why? I had provided all the guidance and mentoring that I could have possibly provide so the next best thing was to "get out of the way."

As I continued to travel throughout the military and as a civilian employee for the federal government, I have often seen leaders that continue to hold on to their leadership positions, preventing the organization from achieving true growth. Don't get me wrong: I am not saying that when you reach a certain age or a true peak in your career that you should immediately step aside. What I am saying is that this is the time where you should be evaluating yourself to see what value-added contributions you are providing to the team and the organization as a whole. There is nothing wrong with stepping to the side and becoming a consultant or mentor within an organization. However, I have seen some organization where the leader just needed to retire, but held on because they felt that the leadership role was a part of them. This sometimes adversely impacts the organization from reaching its true potential.

I have often heard that leaders hold on too long so that others will not forget the historical foundation of the organization. I was in a conversation with a leader and the first thing that came out was that "I have been doing this for thirty-plus years." I followed up with "that is part of the problem if you are not susceptible to change." Again, remember change is not bad. Sometimes it is needed to move the team or organization forward. Instead of boring you with my examples, I think you will get the point after you finish with the tips that I have listed that go directly with this chapter.

Get Out of the Way Tips

When as a Leader do you know it is time to step aside? Before I begin, let me remind you of my definition of leadership. It is about influencing others to accomplish the stated objective(s) of your organization through motivation and actions. Now, I would like to present 10 signs from my perspective of being an active learner of leadership.

1. You have lost your zeal to lead.
2. Decision(s) that you are making are not consistent with the objectives of the organization.
3. You are now the organization instead of being a part of the organization.
4. You have reached your learning capacity (you feel that you know it all and refuse to listen to others).
5. Morale of the organization has plummeted because of your action(s).
6. You have lost connection with the organization (the organization as a whole wants to go one direction, but you want to remain static).
7. You as a leader stop developing your followers (as a military veteran this means you stop or refuse to train your future replacement).
8. You as a leader start questioning or doubting the decision(s) that you make.
9. You demand others to act one way and you as the leader do the opposite.
10. You as leader give up on the ones that need you the most.

Leadership is not about being in charge or simply having positional power. Leadership is the ability to get people to want to do things that they normally would not do. It is about building trust, taking risks to achieve a vision or goal, and being an effective communicator.

6

Bring it All Together

Effective leaders are individuals who are willing to modify their leadership style to influence followers to accomplish a task. Some subordinates respond best to coaxing, suggestions, or gentle prodding; others need and even want at times, the verbal equivalent of a kick in the pants. Treating people fairly doesn't mean treating people as if they were clones of one another. In fact, if you treat everyone the same way, you're probably being unfair, because different people need different things from you.

Leadership can be administered in different ways. The bottom line is successfully influencing individuals to accomplish a given task; that is the work of leading people. I have identified multiple leadership styles: transformational, transactional, cognitive resource theory (directing), and charismatic approach, etc. The most effective leader is willing to tailor their leadership style to the current environment. Remembering that the people whom we lead are our number one commodity; therefore, the leader is the leadership style that they choose when managing and leading employees. Leaders are not limited to any particular leadership style. Effective leaders maximize techniques from various leadership styles to help motivate their subordinates to successful complete the stated objective.

In conjunction with my stated research, there are numerous approaches that can be derived to assist the leadership of any organization to improve. This can be accomplished via the strengthening of the leadership traits developed and learned through understanding of leadership theories. The recommendations will be subdivided into two categories: (I) communicating effectively between the leader and the led and (II) leadership skills training through organizational development and continuing education.

Communicating Effectively

Leaders undoubtedly must be effective communicators with their soldiers on various levels. However, communicating across the military spectrum is a challenge within itself. The majority of organizations must recognize this obstacle and implement methods to reduce the friction. It is helpful to establish a personal and professional presence between all that you lead. Today's society is technologically knowledgeable; therefore, it is an important aspect of leading everyone into the future. With the increased use of this technology, leaders must be aware and supportive of the different methods of communication. Modern technology can help communicate more effectively and prevent communication conflict.

Implementation of effective cross-level communication requires the development of team-building exercises. Forming effective, cohesive small teams is often the first challenge of a leader in a small organization. Nevertheless, the rewards outweigh the challenges; successful teams develop an infectious winner's attitude.

Cohesive teams accomplish missions much more effectively than individuals do. An important thing in leadership in an organization is trust and effective communication. Without some measure of trust and effective communication, nothing will work well. To establish trust, the leader will have to identify areas of common interest and goals and understand the culture in which the organization is functioning. Communicating with the team and keeping them informed also builds trust. According to Gillespie and Mann (2004), "team members' trust in their leader will be positively associated with their ratings of the extra effort they put into their work" (p. 594).

Communication is a necessity in the formula for improving military retention. Communication should exist throughout the organization (strategic) and down to the individual soldiers or small group (tactical). Maintaining an acceptable level of communication within this spectrum reduces the notion that "not being kept informed of important matters" is reduced significantly. Consequently, when there is good communication, leaders have removed yet another major concern for why soldiers leave the military, which is then replaced with justifiable reason to remain on active duty.

Leadership Skill Training through Organizational Development

Leader development is the preparation of leaders through training and education, experience, assessment, counseling, and feedback. Effective organizational leaders grow leaders at all levels of their organization. Leadership development is purposeful, not accidental. Everyday mission requirements are opportunities to grow and develop. Using self-assessments and feedback from subordinates has allowed me to adjust my leadership development plan where needed. An effective leader must understand that leadership development is a continuous process and is both comprehensive and flexible.

Leadership development plans must take into consideration that leaders are inherently followers first and must be technically and tactically proficient to adapt to the changing environment. The tools utilized to complement the leadership development plan are self-development, and job experience gained during operational assignments. These domains interact by using feedback from those that you lead and assessment from various sources. Remembering that effective leaders develop and use power, experience, self-study, and assessment to aid in the ability to influence others. People will follow a leader because of respect and admiration.

BIBLIOGRAPHY

Bass, B. (1990). *Bass & Stogdill's handbook of leadership: Theory, research and managerial applications.* New York: The Free Press.

Bossink, B. (2004). Effectiveness of innovation leadership styles: a manager's influence on ecological innovation in construction projects. *Construction Innovation. 4*(4), p 211-228.

Britt, T. (2003). Black hawk down at work. *Harvard Business Review 81*(1), 16.

Choi, J. (2006). A motivational theory of charismatic leadership: Envisioning, empathy, and empowerment. *Journal of Leadership & Organizational Studies, 13*(1), 24.

Erez, A., Johnson, D., Misangyi, V., & LePine, M. (2008). Stirring the hearts followers: Charismatic leadership as the transferal of affect. *Journal of Applied Psychology, 93*(3), 602-616.

Fiedler, F. (1986). The contribution of cognitive resources to leadership performance. *Journal of Applied Social Psychology 16*, 532-548.

Gillespie, N., and Mann, L. (2004), Transformational leadership and shared values: the building blocks of trust, *Journal of Managerial Psychology*, *19*(6), 588-607. https://doi.org/10.1108/02683940410551507

Gilley, A., Gilley, J., & McMillan, H. (2009). Organizational change: Motivation, communication, and leadership effectiveness. *Performance Improvement Quarterly, 20*(4), 75.

Hackman, J. R., & Wageman, R. (2007). Asking the right questions about leadership Discussion and conclusions. *American Psychologist, 62,* 43-48.

Hersey, P., Blanchard, K., & Johnson, D. (2001). *Management of Organizational Behavior: Leading Human Resources* (8th ed.). Upper Saddle River, NJ: Pearson Prentice Hall.

Kezar, A., Carducci, R., & Contreras-McGavin, M. (2006). *Rethinking the "L" Word in Higher Education: The Revolution of Research on Leadership.* Association for the Study in Higher Education Report, *31*(6). San Francisco, CA: Jossey-Bass.

Kotter, J. (2001). What leaders really do. *Harvard Business Review, (79)*11, 85-96.

Mumford, M., Zaccaro, S., Harding, F., Jacobs, T., & Fleishman, E., (2000). Leadership skills for a changing world: Solving complex social problems. *Leadership Quarterly, 11*(1), 11.

Northouse, P. (2004). *Leadership: Theory and Practice* (3rd ed.). Thousands Oaks, CA: Sage Publication.& Sons.

Yukl, G. (2004). *Leadership in Organizations* (6th ed.). Upper Saddle River, NJ: Pearson Prentice Hall.